E Ellis

History of the Irish Church from the Earliest Days to the

Present Time

E Ellis

History of the Irish Church from the Earliest Days to the Present Time

ISBN/EAN: 9783744726177

Printed in Europe, USA, Canada, Australia, Japan

Cover: Foto ©ninafisch / pixelio.de

More available books at **www.hansebooks.com**

HISTORY ·

OF

THE IRISH CHURCH

FROM ITS EARLIEST DAYS TO THE PRESENT TIME.

BY THE

REV. E. ELLIS, LL.D.

LONDON:

CHRISTIAN BOOK SOCIETY,

22, KING WILLIAM STREET, STRAND.

1869.

HISTORY

OF

THE IRISH CHURCH.

CHAPTER I.

PLANTING THE GOSPEL IN IRELAND.

THE proper description of the Church of England is "the United Church of England and Ireland." When, therefore, we speak of the "Church of England," or the "Church of Ireland," we do so only for convenience of expression, because, properly speaking, there is no "Church of Ireland," or "Church of England" either. When the two countries were united, in the year of our Lord 1800, an Act of Parliament expressly declared that henceforth there should be but *one* Church, to be called "*The United Church of England and Ireland.*"*

* The 5th article of the Act of Union runs thus: "That the Churches of England and Ireland, as now by law established, be united into one Protestant Episcopal Church, to be called the United Church of England and Ireland; and that the doctrine, discipline, and government of said United Church shall be, and shall remain in full force for ever, as the same are now by law established for the Church of England; and that the continuance and preservation of the said United Church, as the Established Church of England and Ireland, shall be deemed and taken to be an essential and fundamental part of the Union."

This is a fact which modern politicians and ultra-Ritualists are most anxious to keep out of sight. The ultra-Ritualist is naturally jealous of the large body of Evangelical clergy which the Irish branch of the United Church boast of, and the politician fears lest the common sense of England should perceive that the case of the Irish Church is only put forth as the thin edge of a wedge which is intended to overthrow the English Establishment.

The agitation against the Irish Church has recently revived, and we have had pastorals and encyclicals from Synods of Romish Bishops in Ireland, and conferences of the Liberation Society in England, all denouncing the oft-threatened Irish Establishment, and assuring us that its days are numbered. But "threatened men live long," and we know that so strong is the case of the Irish Church that the only danger she is in is from the great ignorance which, unfortunately, prevails on the subject.

It may be that some, if not many, persons really fear to think of Ireland's Church history, believing that the Protestant Church there is only an intrusion upon the ancient Popish Church, and was forced upon that country by English arms. Such is a popular notion respecting Ireland; but nothing can be more absurd or incorrect. The object of this history is to set the true facts of the case before the public. And here let us do justice to the Irish character. The people have their faults—great and grievous faults: we speak of the Roman Catholic population; but that they are the victims, and that their faults and miseries are the effects, of Romish misinstruction and superstition, which was forced upon them by England, is equally indisputable.

Ireland was colonized from the East about 1,000 years before Christ, and these early settlers seem to have originally emigrated from Assyria, thence to Phœnicia, then to Spain, out of which they were driven by war and famine, and made their way to Ireland. Traces of this Eastern origin abound in Ireland to this day. The city of Galway still contains numerous ancient buildings after the Spanish model; these are also to be found in other parts of the South and West. These colonists were worshippers of Baal or the Sun, and evidences of their idolatrous worship still present themselves to the observant traveller. Among these the celebrated round towers are commonly thought to have been erected for the exhibition of the sacred fire, while the constant recurrence of the term Balla in the names of places, as Ballinasloe, Ballimena, &c., &c., is simply a corruption of Baal ; the real name of such places being "the City of Baal," "the House of Baal," &c., &c. Again, on St John's-eve (23rd June), a strange relic of Baal-worship may be witnessed in country parts : fires of turf or furze are made across the roads, through which men, women, children, and cattle pass—just as the Assyrians of old are described in the Bible, as causing their children to pass through the brick-kiln to Baal.

It is our purpose to set before our readers, as briefly as possible, an outline of the Ecclesiastical History of Ireland ; and, although historical facts must necessarily occupy a portion of our space, we trust to dispel, in some degree at least, part of the ignorance and misapprehension that prevails, and to show that it has pleased God to preserve, through many troubles and dangers, a faithful Irish Church, holding, in all purity, the faith once delivered to the saints.

I. The Planting of the Gospel in Ireland.

It is a common error to suppose that Christianity was first introduced into Ireland by St. Patrick, A.D. 432, who, as we shall hereafter show, was a thoroughly Christian man, preaching Christ fully, and holding none of the errors of the modern Church of Rome. As in the case of the Churches of England, France, and other countries, there is a difficulty in fixing the precise period at which Christianity was introduced into Ireland, as well as to the quarter from which it comes ; but this is quite clear, from the admissions of Roman Catholic writers, that it was not by Roman agents, or from Rome, that the knowledge of the Lord Jesus came to the sister-isle.

Tertullian, writing in the second century, states that " even those regions of the British isles, where the Roman arms have never yet approached, *are subject to Christ.*" Now, as England and Scotland were brought under the Roman Empire, the passage must apply to Ireland, which was never subject to the Roman arms.

Dr. Lanigan, the Roman Catholic historian, states: " It is universally admitted that there were Christian congregations in Ireland before the mission of Palladius, which took place A.D. 431 " (*i.e.*, the year before St. Patrick); and that " Palladius was the first Bishop sent from Rome to Ireland, to the *Scots believing* in Christ."*

Thus, then, there were Christians in Ireland before the visit of Palladius, Rome's first missionary, who, by the bye, was rejected by the Irish, and who, therefore, in a short stay of less than a year, returned to Rome to report his unsuccessful mission to Pope Celestine.

St. Patrick, in his confession, shows the same fact. Addressing the Irish people, he says, " I journeyed in every direction for your sakes, even to remote places whither no person had ever come to baptize, or to ordain a clergy-

* Eccl. Hist., vol. i. pp. 9, 23.

man." These words clearly imply that some parts, not so distant, had been visited by such persons.

Again, Eusebius, A.D. 325, says that some of the Apostles crossed the ocean to the British isles; and St. Chrysostom, A.D. 390, says, that a person going in his day to the British isles " would hear all men everywhere discoursing matters out of Scriptures." " For even the British isles," he adds, " have felt the power of the Word. There, too, churches and altars have been raised." The words, " British isles," it is needless to observe, would refer no less to Ireland than to England.

It is not altogether improbable that St. Paul preached the Gospel in Britain before the close of the first century. But if the testimony of history renders this probable as regards *England*, other reasons make it specially so, if not more so, respecting *Ireland*. Because, first, the two countries so closely adjoin that there would have been, even in those days, comparatively little obstacle in point of distance. But, secondly, and chiefly (strange as it may sound in the ears of Englishmen in the year 1868), Ireland and its coasts were much better known, and of much greater importance in those days, than England. The trade carried on with Ireland by foreign countries was very great, and thus foreigners could more easily arrive, and intercourse be more regularly sustained, than with the coasts of England. On this point the historian Tacitus, A.D. 97, speaking of Ireland, says: " The soil and climate, and the dispositions and habits of the people, differ not so much from Britain. The approaches to the country and its ports are *better known* through commercial intercourse and merchantmen." *

So much, then, on the introduction of Christianity into

* Agricola, c. 24.

Ireland, which the Church of Rome had no part in, and whose interference was rejected in the person of Palladius by the native Christians. By way of explanation, it may be added that the Irish people were in ancient times commonly known by the name of Scots, or Scottish; and their country by the name of Scotia or Scotland, as well as Hibernia or Ireland; the people of the country now called Scotland being thus designated Albanians, Picts, &c. Bede says of Ireland: " Britain, besides the Britons and the Picts, received a third nation, the Scots, who, departing out of Ireland under their leader Renda, either by fair means or by force of arms, secured to themselves those settlements among the Picts which they still possess. It is properly the country of the Scots, who migrated from thence, as has been said, added a third nation in Britain to the Britons and the Picts."

Elsewhere, also, Bede speaks of " the Scots who inhabit the island of Ireland, which is next to Britain." Mosheim, speaking of the eighth century, " The Irish, or Hibernians, were then called Scots." Archbishop Usher was of the opinion that the country which is now called Scotland did not receive that name until the eleventh century, but had been known by several other names, and especially that of Albania. " This use of the names," says Mr. King, in his " Church History," " continued until very long after Bede's time, and is admitted generally by all writers on the subject of our ancient history."

A very interesting evidence of this is contained in the life of Sulgen, who was Bishop of St. David's about A.D. 1070. He came to Ireland to study, and spent there more than ten years in the study of the Word of God, which facts caused his son John to write the following poem :—

" With ardent love for learning, Sulgen sought
The school in which his fathers had been taught ;
To Ireland's sacred isle he bent his way,
Where science beamed with bright and glorious ray.
But lo ! an unforeseen impediment,
His journey interrupted as he went ;
For sailing toward the country where abode
The people famous in the Word of God,
His bark, by adverse winds and tempests toss'd,
Was forced to anchor on another coast ;
And thus the Albanian shore the traveller gained,
And there for five successive years remained.

* * * * *

At length arriving on the Scottish soil,
He soon applies himself to studious toil ;
The Holy Scriptures now his thoughts engage,
And much he ponders o'er each oft-read page,
Exploring carefully the secret union
Of precious treasure in the law divine ;
Till thirteen years of diligence and pains
Had made him affluent in heavenly gains,
And stored his ample mind with rich supplies
Of costly goods and sacred merchandise.
Then, having gained a literary name,
In high repute for learning home he came,
His gathered store of golden gains to share
Among admiring friends and followers there."

CHAPTER II.

ST. PATRICK.

THE last chapter showed that Christianity was planted in
Ireland totally irrespective of the Church of Rome ; that it
was only in the year A.D. 430 that Pope Celestine sent
Palladius as Bishop to the " Irish believing in Christ," so that

there must have been Christians in Ireland before that year; that Rome's emissary was rejected by the Irish Christians, and he withdrew after about a year's sojourn in Ireland.

In the year following, viz., A.D. 432, St. Patrick came to Ireland. We shall not occupy the time of our readers by narrating all the fables which have been written about him, or the various stories which the Church of Rome has invented, in order the more effectually to delude the poor Roman Catholics of Ireland, especially by trying to induce them to believe that he was the agent of Rome. Indeed, Dr. Lanigan, the Roman Catholic historian, is compelled to admit that "the account of St. Patrick's consecration by Pope Celestine is not to be met with in any of the lives (of the saints), except those two complications of all stories (*i.e.,* fables), namely, Jocelin's and the Tripartite, whence it made its way into some breviaries, and other late documents" (Vol. i , p. 191).

There is much doubt concerning the country of St. Patrick's birth. He was not an Irishman. Some think he was born at Kirkpatrick, in Scotland; others, that he was a native of France, and born at or near Boulogne. It is an unimportant point, yet it may be observed that there are strong reasons for believing that he was a native of Britain. His name originally was "Succath," but this has been lost sight of in the Latin name Patricius, or Patrick. He was born of Christian parents, his father was a deacon in the Church, named Calporneous, and his grandfather was a presbyter, named Potitus. It is, therefore, quite clear that the celibacy of the clergy was not practised in those days; that his father and grandfather were both of them married clergymen, following the example of St. Peter (Matt. viii. 14). Moreover, the novelty of priestly celibacy is admitted by Roman Catholics themselves; for instance, Judge Keogh, an Irish Roman Catholic Judge, in pronouncing judgment in the case of *Beamish* v. *Beamish*, in Four Courts in Dublin, February 20, 1867, said, "*It was not, as some vulgarly supposed, a fact that priests in the Roman Catholic Church were never allowed to marry, that celibacy was always enjoined in the Church. It was a fact that, down to a late period, priests and bishops were allowed to marry, and did marry. To the year* A D. 1015, *priests were allowed to marry ; and the vow of celibacy was not required until the year* 1076."

His native country appears to have been subject to constant invasion by pirates, and when St. Patrick was sixteen years of age he was seized upon by some Irish adventurers, and sold as a slave to a Pagan prince in the north part of the island. "I was brought captive into Ireland," he says, in his " Confession," " for turning astray from God, and for not keeping His commandments."

In his slavery in the county of Antrim, where he was employed in feeding swine, like the prodigal in the parable, he thought upon his ways. His afflictions were blessed to him. "The Lord," he says, " brought me to a sense of the unbelief of my heart : He counselled and comforted me, as a father doth a son."

For about six years he continued in captivity, when he made his escape, and returned to his own country. In the year A.D. 397 he was again carried captive to Ireland, and again, after a short absence, returned. It pleased God, however, to make these sad calamities a blessing, not to Patrick only, but to the very people who so sorely harassed him. Forgetting the injuries they had inflicted, he felt himself called by God to do something for their spiritual welfare.

Love to Christ influenced his heart, and reacted on the souls of Irishmen.

His slavery amongst them had made him acquainted with their language and habits, and now he resolved, by the grace of God, to make known to them the saving truths which he had himself been taught.   To prepare himself for the work, he studied the Bible with the utmost diligence, was ordained in France, and afterwards consecrated as Bishop ; *not* by the Bishop of *Rome*, however, for it is almost certain that St. Patrick was never at Rome.

He was probably sixty years old when he commenced his labours as a missionary in Ireland, and his life was prolonged to a hundred and twenty.   In the year A.D. 432 he landed in county Wicklow, but, as the people did not receive him, he at once proceeded to county Antrim, where he began his work.   In the following year, hearing that the Kings and Parliament of Ireland were about to assemble at the celebrated hill of Tara, he again took shipping, and sailed to the mouth of the Boyne, ascending which he made his way to Tara, where he preached the Gospel with great success.   He afterwards travelled into the west of Ireland, ascended the mountain called Croagh Patrick, from whence, according to the ancient fable, he " *banished all the varmint.*"   For sixty years he laboured zealously throughout Ireland, convincing the people, and arranging matters connected with the Church ; and, having founded the Cathedral of Armagh, he died on the 17th of March, A.D. 492 ; and it is for this reason, it is almost needless to say, that the 17th of March is called St. Patrick's Day.   He was buried at Downpatrick.

Such is a mere outline of the history of this celebrated man.

The Church of Rome tells the poor people of Ireland that

she teaches them the doctrines of St. Patrick. It is, therefore, very important that it should be clearly understood that St. Patrick was not a Papist. Christ Jesus was all his salvation and all his desire. He did not look to or trust in the Virgin Mary, or saints, or angels, but in Jesus his Lord and Saviour. This is evident from his prayer, which he wrote on his way to Tara, supplicating protection and support from on high for the great duties of preaching which there awaited him. It is called his " armour," or " breast-plate," and thus concludes : " Christ," he says, " be with me. Christ before me, Christ after me, Christ in me, Christ under me, Christ over me ; Christ at my right, Christ at my left, Christ at this side, Christ at that side, Christ at my back ; Christ be in the heart of each person I speak to ; Christ in the mouth of each person who speaks to me ; Christ in each eye which sees me ; Christ in each ear which hears me. At Tara to-day I invoke the mighty power of the Trinity. Salvation is the Lord's, salvation is the Lord's, salvation is Christ's. May Thy salvation, O Lord, be always with us ! "

But did not St. Patrick celebrate the sacrifice of the mass ? Certainly not ; he evidently trusted in, and taught the people to rely upon, the once-offered sacrifice of Christ on Calvary. This is easy of proof. It is well known that a Popish priest can only offer his so-called sacrifice of the mass on a stone altar. Hence, the ultra-Ritualistic " priest," in his puerile imitation of the mass, begins by introducing a stone altar into the Church of England, contrary to the law. As long as the Irish Church continues independent of Rome, *wooden altars* alone were used. The *first* appointed English Archbishop of Dublin, John Comyn, was the *first* who had a canon made at the Synod of Dublin, A.D. 1186, " *forbidding priests to celebrate mass on wooden altars, according to the usage of*

Ireland." On this canon, Dr. Lanigan, the Roman Catholic historian remarks, that *" before the time of Constantine the Great, the Christian altars or holy tables were generally made of wood ;"* and he adds, *" It is not, therefore, to be wondered at, that the Irish made their altars of wood from the beginning, and that they continued to do so in consequence of their attachment to the pratices received from St. Patrick "* (Eccl. Hist., iv. 272).

Take another view of St. Patrick's opinions, as opposed to those of Rome. The Word of God was his chief delight. It was the subject of his constant study in private, and teaching in public ; so much so, that an early Roman Catholic writer (Joceline) says : " He used to read the Bible to the people, and explain it to them, for days and nights together." Who ever heard of a Roman Catholic priest doing so in modern times?

Again : St. Patrick did not trust to his own merits for salvation. " I was a stone," he says, " which lies in the deep mire ; and He who is mighty came and, in His mercy, raised me out of it. What shall I say or promise to the Lord ? For I possess no strength but what He hath given me. From God I have received to be what I am."

Again : St. Patrick did not believe that clergymen should necessarily be unmarried, as the Church of Rome teaches. One of his canons enacted a penalty against the wife of any clergyman who should venture out of doors without having her head veiled. Whatever we may think of the canon, it certainly proves that he was not a member of that apostasy which " forbids to marry."

Neither did St. Patrick believe in the propriety of prayers for the dead, for he writes: " Give not that which is holy unto dogs ; for he who in his lifetime will not deserve to receive the sacrifice, how can it help him after his death ? '

Space, however, will not permit to dwell further on the history of this great man, on whose labours in Ireland the Divine blessing was remarkably vouchsafed. Through his instrumentality, the Gospel of Christ was embraced by very many of the natives who had previously resisted or neglected. it. In short, although Christianity had a footing in the country before, it seems now to have taken root more deeply, and to have gained an influence almost universal, upon the minds and affections of the people.

These details of St Patrick's doctrines and labours convincingly prove that neither "Ireland's Apostle," nor any of the founders of the Irish Church, held the erroneous doctrines of the modern Church of Rome.

CHAPTER III.

EARLY IRISH CHURCH INDEPENDENT OF ROME.

THE IRISH CHURCH CONTINUED INDEPENDENT OF ROME, AND WAS MADE A BLESSING TO ENGLAND, SCOTLAND, AND OTHER COUNTRIES OF EUROPE.

This is a startling assertion, and doubtless sounds strange in the ears of Englishmen. Some will scarcely bring themselves to believe that England was ever indebted to Ireland for Scriptural truth. But so it was; and historical facts recorded by English historians put the matter beyond a doubt.

It is needful here to say something about monasteries. In these days we have such a thorough and wholesome dread of such establishments, that it is somewhat hard to believe they ever were wholesome and good. They are in our day seminaries of idolatry and superstition, and, too often, chambers of immorality, conspiracy, and treason. Far different, how-ever, was their character in the early period of British and Irish history, of which we are writing, while as yet the Church was independent of Rome. The study of the Bible, as well as the teaching and preaching of the truth as it is in Jesus, both within and without the walls, were the high and holy purposes for which they were established. Churches were very scarce, and these monasteries supplied their place. Moreover, they formed centres of missionary labours. When a man of God came into a neighbourhood where Jesus was unknown, he fixed on a central spot, as regards the people. There he built a monastery, and from hence these servants of Christ went everywhere preaching the Word. " *Our monas-teries in ancient times,*" says the good Archbishop Usher, "*were the seminaries of the ministry, being, as it were, so many colleges of learned divines, whereunto the people did usually resort for instruction, and from whence the Church was wont to be supplied with able ministers.*"

It is a fact, too, established on undoubted testimony, that the Irish were famous for learning. Mosheim, the well-known Church historian, says : " *That the Hibernians were lovers of learning, and distinguished themselves in those times of ignorance by the culture of the sciences beyond all other European nations, travelling through the most distant lands, is a fact with which I have long been acquainted ; as we see them discharging with the highest reputation the function of doctors in France, Germany, and Italy during both the eighth and ninth centuries.*"

Hospitality then, as now, distinguished the Irish. The English historian, Bede (iii. 27), tells us that about A.D. 661 a pestilence broke out in Britain, and carried off great num-bers ; that it spread to Ireland, and adds that " many of the nobility and lower ranks of the English nation were there at the time, having retired thither either for study of the Word of God, or else to observe a stricter life.   All of whom the Scots (*i. e.*, the Irish) received most cordially, and provided them with daily bread, with books, and with instruction, *free of charge.*"

Among other eminent persons who resorted to Ireland was the celebrated Alfrid, King of Northumberland, of whom Bede tells us "*he lived as a sojourner in the country of the Scots (i. e., Irish), and there imbibed heavenly wisdom with all his heart's attention, for he had left his native land to learn in studious exile the mysteries of the Lord.*"

King Alfrid spent his time in county Mayo, and when he returned to England he brought with him some Irish divines, by whose aid he afterwards, it is said, founded the University of Oxford.

In secular affairs, too, Ireland seems to have taken the lead of the rest of Europe, so long as her Church was unconnected with the Pope of Rome.   For instance, justice was so admirably administered, that an anecdote is told of a beautiful young lady, adorned with jewels, who, with a wand only in her hand, at the top of which was a valuable ring, walked alone through the length and breadth of Ireland unmolested*—a story which has suggested Moore's beautiful ballad, of which we venture to give two or three verses :—

> " Rich and rare were the gems she wore,
>   And a bright gold ring on her wand she bore ;
> But oh ! her beauty was far beyond
>   Her sparkling gems, or snow-white wand.

---

* Warner's " History of Ireland," vol. i. Book x.

"Lady! dost thou not fear to stray,
    So lone and lovely, through this bleak way?
Are Erin's sons so good, or so cold,
    As not to be tempted by women or gold?

*   *   *   *   *

"On she went, and her maiden smile
    In safety lighted her round the Green Isle;
And blest for ever is she who relied
    Upon Erin's honour, and Erin's pride."

The pay of the judges was a fat hog from each townland which they visited; and it provokes a smile to think of a Lord Chancellor driving home a herd of swine, the fees given him on circuit.

Agriculture, though perhaps as forward as in any other part of Europe, had not made much progress. The ploughing, for instance, was accomplished by tying the horses' tails to the plough. Ireland boasted, too, of a militia, the qualifications for which were rather high. A militiaman must be a good poet, be able to leap as high as his head, and be ready to fight ten men of any nation, single-handed.

But Ireland's principal glory at the time referred to was the extraordinary missionary spirit exhibited by her sons, and which led them to preach the pure Gospel of Christ during the leaden ages in almost every country in Europe, the details of which are much too interesting to be crowded into a corner; they are, therefore, reserved for the next chapter.

CHAPTER IV.

THE EARLY IRISH CHURCH A BLESSING TO CHRISTENDOM.

ANCIENT church histories clearly show that the Irish Church not only flourished itself as a pure Christian Church, independent of Rome, but also that it was a means of blessing England, Scotland,. and other countries, with the light of the Gospel of Christ, and that at a time when Christendom was so engrossed with Papal darkness as caused that period to be termed the leaden age.

It is a fact, established almost unanimously by ancient authors, that the Irish people, even long before the eighth century, were eminent for the cultivation of letters, philosophy, and sacred literature ; and so numerous were the schools, colleges, and other seminaries of learning, that the country was a kind of university in itself, to which students flocked in great numbers from all parts, in order to enjoy the superior instruction, especially in theology, which Ireland then afforded ; and so highly valued was that instruction, and so celebrated was the country for the number and excellence of its learned and holy men, that Ireland was known as the " Sacred Isle," or the " Isle of Saints." They were, however, not such as Popish saints, but saints indeed, after the Bible fashion—faithful, devoted, self-denying men of God, who were mighty in the Scriptures, mighty in prayer, and ever engaged in works of faith and labours of love.

The two leading causes of the preference which was then given to an Irish education were these : First, the admirable and superior discipline which was observed in its colleges ; and, secondly (yet chiefly), the immense knowledge of the Word of God which the Irish instructors possessed, and the ability and excellence of their teaching.

The English embraced the benefit and blessing of the superior religious education Ireland afforded to her youth. If space permitted, the English historian, Bede, might be largely quoted respecting the labours and success of the Irish missionaries in this country. Suffice it to say, that he speaks of

the excellence of their character, the Christian simplicity of
their habits, their indefatigable exertions in preaching the
Word of God, and the delight with which our forefathers
flocked to hear them. "Whenever any of these missions
aries," he says (iii. 36), "came into a village, the villagers
immediately assembled together, and entreated him to ad-
minister to them the Word of Life."

In SCOTLAND so important were the labours of the Irish
missionaries, that an Irishman, the famous Columba, was
called the "Apostle of the Highlands and Western Isles of
Scotland." He is better known by the name of Columbkille—*i.e.*, St. Columb of the Churches, from the great number of churches and monasteries which he founded, for the
word "kille" means church. This energetic man, who was
a member of the royal family of Ireland, was born A.D. 521.
He founded the city of Londonderry by establishing the
monastery of Doire (or Derry) Calgaich, the word Derry
signifying the "*place of oaks*," from which that celebrated
town derives its name. It was afterwards called London-
derry, because the city was colonized by a party of London
adventurers.

After labouring for some time in Ireland, Columbkille,
hearing that the isles and northern parts of Scotland were
sunk in heathen darkness and Druidical superstition, went
thither in A.D. 563, and founded a monastery in the island
of Iona. Great success attended his labours among the
Picts; for in a few years the greater part of the Highlands
was brought to the knowledge of the Gospel, and the gross
superstitions of Druidism were abolished.

Columba settled on one of the New Hebrides, named Iona,
where he founded the monastery of Columba, the ruins of
which still remain, and are kept in excellent order by the

liberality of the noble proprietor, the Duke of Argyle. In 1820 and 1823 Iona was visited by the Rev. Legh Richmond (see his Memoir, pp. 302, &c.), who tells us that—

'*Iona now contains only one village, with mean houses, and about* 400 *inhabitants. It is the most noted place of Caledonian antiquity. . . . St. Columba came from Ireland to Iona in the sixth century. . . . The college founded by Columba was the seat and centre of literature and piety; and from thence these blessings were diffused, not only over the British islands, but throughout the greater part of Europe. Iona is the burial-place of forty-eight Scotch crowned heads, four Irish kings, eight Norwegian princes, and a multitude of nobility and religious orders. It had also* 360 *crosses, which were destroyed, except one, at the Reformation. The ruin of the once splendid cathedral cannot fail to interest the traveller, and to excite the deepest emotions in the heart of the Christian.*'

So much for the influence of Irish Christianity in England and Scotland; while if we turn to the Continent of Europe, we find almost everywhere traces of the Irish missionary work. In Switzerland, Gallus, an Irishman, laboured so zealously and sucessfully that an ancient work ("Nother's Martyrology") says of him: "*Divine mercy raised up blessed Gallus to be the apostle of the Alemannic people. He was himself experienced in the ways of God, and finding the people enveloped in Paganism, he instructed them in the true faith, and brought them out of the darkness of ignorance to the sun of righteousness, which is Christ.*" Few of the numerous English tourists who every season visit the town and abbey of St. Gall, remember that the place was named after the devoted Irishman.

Killian also, the favoured Irish bishop and martyr,

flourished in the seventh century, and was called the Apostle of Franconia—that is, the country inhabited by the Eastern Franks, many of whom were, by his means, converted from Paganism to Christianity. Like John the Baptist of old, he reproved the chief ruler of the country for marrying his brother's wife. He met with a similar fate, the enraged woman having procured his assassination.

But of all the eminent Irishmen who, at the period we are writing of, honoured their native land, and as Christian missionaries gladdened the hearts of heathen foreigners, by far the most celebrated was Columbanus, noted especially as one " mighty in the Scriptures." He settled in Burgundy, where he founded monasteries, and zealously preached the Gospel to the barbarous and depraved people. Providential circumstances caused him to move frequently from one place to another. France, Switzerland, and Italy were some of the scenes of his energetic and pious labours. From his writings it is evident that he was no Papist; and so far from believing the infallibility of Popes, he held that Pope Vigilius died a heretic.

Passing on to the eighth century, we have a curious example of the superior knowledge which was then possessed by Irishmen over their English contemporaries.

The celebrated Virgil, Bishop of Saltzburg, was an Irishman. He and an eminent English missionary, named Boniface, were at the same time labouring among the heathen tribes in Germany. Boniface was the Pope's missionary, and attached to the Papal cause; whereas Virgil was an independent missionary, attached to the doctrine and discipline of the ancient Church of Ireland.

A dispute soon rose between them, and Boniface wrote to the Pope, charging Virgil with errors in Catholic doctrine.

The heaviest charge made against the Irish missionary was, that he said *that the earth was round*, and that there was another world at the other side, and men walking on the earth: "Even," said he to Boniface, "under the place where you now stand!" Boniface, though an English missionary, and in high favour with the Pope of Rome, had never before heard that which almost every child in our schools knows— namely, that the earth is round. A Roman Catholic, who believes his' Pope *infallible*, would feel quite satisfied that the answer to the complaint shows that "His Holiness" knew at least as much as the little children in our National Schools. But the Pope knew no more than his missionary, and not half so much as the despised missionary of Ireland. "As for the perverse and wicked doctrine," he wrote, "of that man who has spoken against God and his own soul, if it is certain that he holds such an opinion as that there is another world, and other men, under the earth, or a sun and moon there, assemble a Council, degrade him from the priesthood, and expel him from the Church."

Thus, then, it is clear that, during those ages, which, from the ignorance and superstition that prevailed in Europe, have been termed the *leaden* ages, the Church in Ireland was as a lighthouse, shedding abroad bright beams of knowledge and Scriptural truth, and illuminating the nations with the glorious Gospel of Jesus Christ.

And now that much honoured Church, still true to her Master, is to be disendowed to pleasure the apostate Church of Rome, unless English Protestants rise up and say that they are not prepared to sacrifice a sister Protestant Church at the bidding of those who hate the true Gospel, and keep away God's Word from the people.

CHAPTER V.

HOW AND WHEN IRELAND'S ANCIENT CHURCH BECAME SUBJECT TO THE CHURCH OF ROME.

IT is necessary that the reader should bear in mind the
proofs already given, showing that more than a thousand
years ago the Church of Ireland was the burning and shining
light of Christendom.   Her candlestick was seen from afar,
diffusing its rays like a luminous beacon of some lofty lighthouse planted on a rock amid the foaming surge of the ocean,
and casting its light on the dark sea to guide the mariner in
his course.   Such was the Church of Ireland then.   Such
she was specially to England.   As Englishmen, we ought not
to endeavour to conceal our obligations to her.   English
Christians ought not to be ashamed to confess that with regard to learning, and especially with regard to sacred literature, Ireland was in advance of England at that time.   The
sons of England's kings, nobles, and gentry, were sent for
education thither.   Ireland was the university of the west of
Europe.   She was rich in libraries, colleges, and schools.
She was famous, as now, for hospitality.   She received
those who came to her with affectionate generosity, and
provided them with books and instructors.   She trained them
in sound knowledge, especially in the Word of God.

Nor was this all.   We showed our readers that the Christianity of England and Scotland, was, in a great measure,
reflected upon them by Irish missionaries who came from the
Scriptural school of Iona, which was founded in the sixth
century by St. Columba, a descendant of Ireland's ancient kings.

During all this time the Church of Ireland continued
perfectly independent of the Church of Rome, which was

gradually becoming clouded with errors, and losing sight of the written Word as the alone rule of faith. England, too, was gradually being brought under the Pope, and points of dispute sprung up between the Churches of England and Ireland. These points of dispute were, some of them, unimportant. One was as to the time of observing Easter, there being a difference of one day. The other was as to the tonsure, *i.e.*, the manner in which her priests' heads should be shaved. These are trifling subjects to engage the attention of divines, and so thought some, even in those days; for a Romish writer (Mabillon) says of them, "a question about one day then occupied the Church for nearly 600 years, and three centuries at least were scarcely sufficient for settling the hair of quarrelsome men."

The real point at issue was, the Church of Rome was ambitious, and desired to bring all the Churches of Christendom into subjection to herself; and these points respecting Easter and the tonsure were as the thin edge of the wedge by which she thought to enslave the native Churches. The old Scriptural Churches of England and Ireland saw that their independence was at stake, and therefore resisted Romish efforts to enslave them. They desired "union in essentials, liberty in non-essentials, and charity in all things."

The English however were gradually brought under Rome, but not so the Irish. True to their ancient Church, they resolutely refused to sell their liberty; and therefore, when artifices had failed, the Church of Rome had recourse to curses. Accordingly we find writers, even as late as the twelfth century, speaking of the Irish as "barbarous," "ungodly," "stiff-necked," "wolves," "worse than wild beasts," "great heretics," "flesh-eaters in Lent," &c.

We can now imagine some of our intelligent readers asking

—If this be so, how and when did Ireland's ancient Church resign her liberty ? How and when did priests of a foreign faith come to her shores ? How and when did Irish Catholics bow down at the knee of an Italian Bishop ? The answer is simple. In the ninth century Ireland was invaded by the Danes, who made great havoc. They pillaged and burnt churches, libraries, and schools, and slew many of the clergy. For two hundred years these invasions continued, the Danes pouring their innumerable swarms into Ireland, whose ancient kings and princes, with persevering valour, repelled their incursions.

At length, after two centuries of war and bloodshed, the celebrated battle of Clontarf, near Dublin, was fought in 1014 A.D., when the old Irish hero, Brian Boru, in a signal victory, crushed the Danish forces, while he himself perished in the fight. But, though vanquished, the Danes were permitted to settle in three towns in Ireland, namely, Dublin, Waterford, and Limerick. Before this the Saxons and Danes had conquered England ; and now, in this century, A.D. 1066, the Norman Conquest took place, and the Papal power was fully established in England. The Danes settled in Ireland claimed affinity with the Normans, and applied to have their bishops consecrated by the English Primate. Accordingly a bishop was consecrated by the Archbishop of Canterbury for the Danes in Dublin, A.D. 1074 ; *and thus the very first point of the wedge of Rome's authority was through England introduced into the sister country.*

The Irish Church, however, still maintained its independence, and therefore Rome eagerly watched for an opportunity of bringing it under her power ; nor had she long to wait, for King Henry II., wishing to seize upon Ireland, applied to Pope Adrian IV., whose real name was Nicholas Breakspear, the only Englishman that ever occupied the Papal chair, for his sanction, promising that *he would not only bring the Irish within the pale of the Romish Church,* but would pay the Pope a penny a year (Peter's pence) for every house in Ireland. Adrian, as our readers may suppose, made not the least objection, and gave the English king permission to seize Ireland.

At this time the kingdom of Meath was governed by a base and profligate king, whose name was Dermod M'Morogh, who had forcibly carried off the wife of another prince. The King of Ireland rescued the captive princess, and took vengeance on Dermod by desolating his kingdom. Dermod fled to Henry and promised, that if restored to his kingdom by English arms, he would hold it as a vassal of the English king.

So far, then, Henry's way seemed plain ; but he was just then occupied in a war with France, besides being engaged in perplexing disputes with Thomas à Becket, Archbishop of Canterbury, and so unable to go in person to Ireland. A strong force was, however, despatched under Richard Strong-bow, Earl of Pembroke, in A.D. 1169. The Earl sailed up the river Suir, in order to attack Waterford, and while on his passage up the river an incident occurred which is said to have given rise to a well-known proverb. He suddenly found his progress opposed by two strong forts, one on each side of the river ; the one was called Hook, and the other Crook. Some of his captains asked how he would possibly get up to Waterford, when the Earl replied that get there he would, *"either by Hook or by Crook."* · English arms prevailed, and such was the progress made by the forces that in 1171 Henry himself went over, and all the native princes, except one, submitted to the English king.

Henry having thus secured Ireland, was faithful to his

engagement with the Pope.   Under his direction, there was
held, A.D. 1172, the *Synod of Cashel,* where it was decreed
" *That for the future all divine offices be performed in all
parts of the Church of Ireland after the likeness of most
Holy Church, according to the rule the Anglican Church
observeth.*"   Alas, for the Church of Ireland! her glory set,
her liberty departed.*

Thus, then, Popery was forced upon Ireland by British
arms ; and the Irish Church, which had formerly been a burning and a shining light, casting the bright beams of the
Gospel upon the world, became idolatrous and superstitious,
subject to the Pope of Rome, and continued in captivity for
a period of about 365 years.

While these statements of Irish Church history are being
written, we are reminded how they are illustrated by, and, in
a sense, mixed up with things that are just going on around
us.   For instance, referring to the visit recently paid by the
Prince and Princess of Wales to Ireland,† we read in the
Times, that their Royal Highnesses have attended Divine
service in Christ Church, a cathedral of historic interest, as-
sociated with the record of stormy events and the career of
great warriors from a period of remote antiquity.   To the
princess especially it presented an interesting and suggestive
memorial of the wonderful advancement of the great kingdom
with which her own destiny is linked, and of the vicissitudes
of the gallant country which gave her birth.   Christ Church
is altogether Danish in its origin.   It was one of the first
institutions which sprang into existence after the enterprising

* MS. of Giraldus Cambrinsis, F. 4. 4. (in library of Trinity
College, Dublin), p. 24, transcribed by King in Ch. Hist. Appendix,
No. xxxvi. p. 1054—5.

† May, 1868.

courage of the famous Northmen had established their dominion over this land more securely than was usual in those ages of precarious conquest. It was founded 830 years ago by a Danish king and a Danish bishop. Among the monuments which adorn its venerable isle is that of the famous Strongbow, who, as we have shown above, commanded the English forces which conquered Ireland. Strongbow was the intrepid foe of the Danes, whose struggles to retain even a remnant of their hard-bought acquisitions evinced the same heroic qualities in that age which have in recent times won for them the sympathy of Europe while resisting unjust aggression.

Here, too, is deposited a venerable trophy in the shrine of St. Cubic, carried away from England by a marauding expedition of the citizens of Dublin in support of the cause of King Henry IV., when a rebellion was excited by the Duke of Northumberland. The King was not forgetful of those services, but evinced his gratitude by allowing the Lord Mayor of Dublin to assume, among his paraphernalia of civic state, a sword such as the Lord Mayor of London had borne before him.

In the feuds of the Geraldines and Ormondes, Christ Church was appointed as a place to make atonement by the citizens for taking part with the Fitzgeralds. Here the Mayor did penance by going barefoot to the gates. There are few epochs in the history of the Anglo-Irish settlement and the vicissitudes of British rule in Ireland with which some link may not be found attached to the old Christ's Church Cathedral in Dublin.

CHAPTER VI.

THE FRUITS OF POPERY IN IRELAND.

HAVING seen how Ireland's old Scriptural Church was
brought under the tyranny of the Pope of Rome, by the
instrumentality of Englishmen, in the year of our Lord 1172,
this chapter is devoted to show what effects the introduction
of Popery had on the clergy, laity, and country at large.

Romish errors were now generally adopted in Ireland, and
the Irish Church, which, as our readers have seen, had been
formerly a burning and a shining light, casting the bright
beams of the Gospel upon the world, lost its love for the
Scripture, and, Roman-like, took up with the traditions of
men.

Scriptural faith is the true and only root of Scriptural
morality. Immorality, depravity, and a general decay in
holiness and purity, are the necessary results of decay in
faith, which purifieth the heart, and in Bible knowledge,
which maketh wise unto salvation. No person need, therefore, be surprised to learn that the Church of Ireland, having
become corrupt in *doctrine*, became corrupt in *practice also.*
The clergy became profligate and ignorant ; so astonishing
was their degradation in point of learning, that history
(Mant i. 33) uses these words concerning them : "The
Irish priests themselves were not able to say mass, or pro-
nounce the words, not knowing what they themselves say in
the Roman tongue." And an old writer, who is quoted both
for the sake of his testimony, as well as to give a sample of
English spelling in those days, says : "Amongst the many
causes of the mysseordor of the land, there is no arche-
bysshop, no bysshop, abbot no pryor, parson no vycar, no any

other person of the Church, high or low, that useth to preach the worde of Godde."

Here we give one sample of the unchristian-like character of the clergy of the period, containing one of the old legends of Christ's Church Cathedral, to which we referred in the last chapter.

A violent although clever Englishman, of the name of Cumin, was appointed Archbishop of Dublin by the King of England. Soon afterwards, some of his lands were seized by the avaricious Lord Deputy of the time. The archbishop was enraged, and resolved on vengeance. He laid the City of Dublin under what is called an *interdict*, a Romish means of torturing the feelings of the superstitious, for while it lasts no Church rite is allowed; no mass, no marriages, no prayers; but the churches were closed against the living, and the corpses of the dead were buried, like dogs, in the roads and ditches, without prayers or religious ceremony.

Not content with this, in order to induce the superstitious people to believe that the affliction which he endured was actually an affliction *to Christ*, and that, by means of it, Christ's sufferings upon the cross had been renewed, he laid all the crucifixes in Christ's Church Cathedral prostrate on the ground, with crowns of thorns on the heads of the images. One of the figures, he said, was a miraculous representation of the suffering Saviour; and, by a little skill, he contrived to present the face of that image as inflamed, its eyes as shedding tears, its body as bathed in sweat, and its side as pouring forth blood and water !

Such was the indecent and blasphemous conduct of this Roman Catholic Archbishop.

And " like priest, like people," sad scenes of anarchy and bloodshed prevailed. The case of the Earl of Kildare may be quoted as an example. This nobleman was accused of many great and heinous crimes, and cited to appear before the King and his Council in London to be tried. Before his trial began the King said to the Earl, that as he was accused of very serious crimes, affecting his life, he had better select some learned counsel to defend him. The Earl, with the ready wit of an Irishman, replied, that he would select the cleverest man in all England, for, said he, " I will have your Grace for my counsel "—a piece of flattery which pleased the King. During the trial he was accused of having burned down the Cathedral of Cashel. Nothing abashed, the Earl admitted that he had done so ; " but," added he, " I assure your Grace that I would not have burned the church, had I not believed that the Archbishop was inside." In the end he was acquitted, and sent back to Ireland as Lord Deputy.

In confirmation of this story, we may add that if any of our readers visit the Tower of London they may see on the walls of the Beauchamp Tower the coat of arms, &c., of this nobleman carved by himself during his imprisonment.

Nor was this all : the Church of Rome not unfrequently appointed laymen, and even children, to benefices in the Church. An old Romish author * says of Bishops of his time : " *They thrust men into holy orders that are like a company of jackdaws ; infamous boys and illiterate, such as are not fit for anything else, and are not called by God, contrary to the rules of our forefathers ; yet if any suffer a repulse he flies to Rome, where the most holy fathers admit hostlers, cooks, and idiots to the altars of the great God. Surely they must have evil thoughts of religion and themselves, or design to abuse Christian people, who do such things—the tree is known by its fruit.*"

* " Aventinus Annales," II. p. 118, *scr. circa,* A.D. 1500.

In inquiring what were the fruits of the Roman Catholic Church establishment in Ireland for 365 years, between the twelfth and sixteenth centuries, we need not dwell on the rapacious extortion and exactions by Rome of Roman Legates in Ireland ; nor on the collations by Rome of Irish bishoprics and other dignities on Italians, sometimes on boys and absentees ; or on the vast treasure drawn out of Ireland to Rome at that time. We will pass by these, and refer to two remarkable public documents, which exhibit in clear light the effects of Popery in Ireland at that period.

The first of these is a petition of the Roman Catholic nobles of Ireland to Pope John XII., in the reign of Edward II. of England, in the year 1318.

In it the petitioners complain that Pope Hadrian IV., being an Englishman and swayed by English partialities, had given Ireland to England, and that Ireland had been plundered by English settlers, who had invaded under pretence of zeal for religion. They complain that, in the administration of law, invidious distinctions were made ; that if an Englishman kills an Irishman no penalty is inflicted on the murderer, and that the murderer is treated with honour by the English, even by English Bishops (who, be it remembered, were nominated or approved by Rome) ; and that it is a doctrine publicly taught by those English ecclesiastics in Ireland (who were all Roman Catholic Prelates), that it is no greater crime to kill an Irishman than it is to kill a dog, and that no one of Irish blood ought to be received as a member of any English religious house in Ireland ; that in consequence of these rigorous enactments and cruel outrages civil feuds have raged in Ireland since the grant of Ireland to England by the Pope, and that during that period 50,000 persons have been murdered by the sword, &c.

D

The second document is called " the Statute of Kilkenny," made by English Roman Catholic bishops, nobles, and others in the Parliament of Ireland, A.D. 1367.

This Act decreed, amongst other things, that no Irishman resident among the English should use the Irish language, his own native tongue. Englishmen were not permitted to allow the cattle of Irishmen to graze on their lands. It was even prescribed by Act of Parliament that the English were to wear a differently cut whisker from the Irish, and he who wore the Irish-cut beard was thereby known to be an enemy and traitor. In a word, the tendency of these statutes was to perpetuate the hatred between the Irish Roman Catholics and the English Roman Catholics in Ireland.

The question here is, Did the Pope intervene to redress these grievances ? Did he mediate between the two parties, both of which were Roman Catholics and acknowledged his supremacy ? Did he say, like the Hebrew leader of old, " Sirs, ye are brethren ; why do ye wrong one to another ? " No, he did not. On the contrary, the Roman Catholic Bishops of Ireland accepted this un-christian statute, and many of them pledged themselves to excommunicate those who violated it.

Such were the results of Romish supremacy in Ireland. The whole period of Roman ascendancy in Ireland, that is to say, the interval between Henry II. and Henry VIII., was a period of deadly feuds. The state was torn by discord, and the Church was rent asunder by schism. Nominally, there was one Church in Ireland—the Church of Rome. But, in fact, there were *two Churches* in Ireland, though both owned the supremacy of Rome. These were the Native Irish Church and the Anglo-Roman Church, and these regarded each other with feelings of mortal hate. The bitter fruits of this war of race against race remain to this day.

CHAPTER VII.

THE REFORMATION.

In the early part of this work we laid down that there were three great epochs in Irish Church history—First, the long period of her independence of the Church of Rome, under whose sway she only came in A.D. 1172; secondly, the period during which she lay under the Roman yoke, extending over 365 years; and thirdly, the time which has elapsed since the Reformation, when she cast off Popish supremacy, and came back to her original purity of faith and practice.

It is with the last of these periods we now have to deal. The sad effects which followed the reception of Romish doctrine have been seen; how the clergy, so long celebrated for learning and piety, became ignorant and dissolute; the people rebellious and bloodthirsty, and the country generally ruined and demoralized. Nor let it be imagined that these statements rest on Protestant authorities. The celebrated Cardinal Bellarmine reluctantly admits, when speaking of the state of the Church before the Reformation. "*For some years before the Lutheran and Calvinistic heresies were published, there was not (as contemporary authors testify) any severity in ecclesiastical jurisdiction, any discipline with regard to morals, any knowledge of sacred literature, any reverence for Divine things; there was almost no religion remaining.*" *

Who will say, in the face of such a statement as this, that there was not need of a reformation, our enemies themselves being judges?

* Bellar. Concio xxviii., Oper. tom. vi., Col. 296, edit. Colon. 161

Our readers have already seen how Ireland became subject to England in the reign of Henry II. We have given the history briefly, but it must not be supposed that the nation were indifferent to the change. Quite the contrary, and among other evidences of its strong feeling we find that a synod was convened, in which it was proposed as a question for deliberation: Why had it pleased God to afflict Ireland, and to bring her into bondage to English strangers? It was declared, in reply, by the Council, that these calamities had fallen upon her as a chastisement for her iniquities in encouraging the slave trade, especially by the purchase of slaves stolen from England.* This traffic had been carried on for many years. St Patrick himself in his youth (as we have seen) had been kidnapped, and sold into Ireland as a slave, probably from Britain. It was a righteous retribution of Divine Providence that they who had enslaved others should be reduced to slavery, and that they should be enslaved by that nation whose children they had bought as slaves.

We need not remind our English readers that the English Reformation commenced by King Henry VIII. throwing off the Papal supremacy. A celebrated man named Brown, a great reformer was made Archbishop of Dublin, and under his influence the Irish Parliament, consisting entirely of Roman Catholics, abolished the Pope's supremacy in Ireland.

The Irish Parliament declared by its Acts that "the King of England, his heirs and successors, was the supreme head on earth of the Church of Ireland." The Acts were opposed by the bishops, but all the Irish princes declared their determination to rout the Pope's power out of the country, so sickened were they of him and his fatal system.

* See Occasional Sermons by Canon Wordsworth, p. 103.

The Pope stirred up rebellion upon more than one occasion, but it was defeated. And by a Bull, dated August 31st, 1535, he cursed Henry King of England, and consigned him " *to eternal damnation.*"

Henry was succeeded by the young Edward VI. In his short reign some progress, but not much, was made. Bishops were appointed who desired reformation, and the noble Liturgy of England was introduced to the Church of Ireland. This last step caused great indignation amongst the Pope's friends.

The Archbishop of Armagh, *e. g.*, being grieved at the abolition of the *Latin* service, said of our Prayer-book, " Oh, every unlearned fellow will be able to say mass for himself now !" This was intended as a slight, but it was in reality an honourable testimony to the English Liturgy; for ours is most truly a " *Common* Prayer-book." So simple, that all can understand it; so heavenly in its expression, that all may be truly edified.

Edward VI. was succeeded by the Bloody Mary upon the British throne. Our readers know the dreadful results in England. Of course the Reformation in Ireland also was for a time at an end. Popery was again established in that country. The Reformed Bishops were deprived of their sees, Romish Prelates were appointed, and the Pope's supremacy was restored by Act of Parliament.

Some will ask, however, " Were not the Irish Protestants *persecuted ?*" They *were*, but not by any means to the same extent as in England. *Not* that Mary wished to spare them, but the savage persecution in England too much occupied her attention. Besides which the Protestants of Ireland were more loyal to the British Crown than the Papists, and could therefore be ill spared.

But after some time the murderous decree went forth which was intended to consign them to the flames. An act was passed whereby all the Protestants of Ireland were liable to be burnt. Mary signed the commission authorizing their destruction, and gave it to the Dean of St. Paul's, directing him to take it to Dublin.

But God had mercy upon Ireland, and, in a way most wonderful, interposed and saved its afflicted people. The Dean started for Dublin; and while he rested at an inn in Chester, was waited upon by the Mayor of that town. He was full of joy at the prospect of a Protestant Massacre in Ireland, and it formed the subject of conversation with his visitor; even in the presence of the woman (Elizabeth Edmonds) to whom the hotel belonged. This woman was a Protestant, and had a brother of the same religion in Dublin. She was therefore greatly distressed when the Dean took out of a small box, which he carried in his bag, a paper signed by the Queen, and shouted with ecstacy, " Here is a commission that shall lash the Protestant heretics of Ireland ! "

She watched her opportunity, and, while the Mayor took leave, and the Dean complimented him downstairs, she opened the box, took out the paper, and put instead of it a pack of cards, with the knave of clubs uppermost, wrapped up in a sheet of paper. The Dean, suspecting nothing, went on to Dublin, told his business to the Lord-Deputy, who summoned a full council to receive the Queen's commands. But, of course, the paper was gone ! The Dean looked very foolish, but declared that he had received a commission. " Go back for another," cried the Lord-Deputy, " and meanwhile we will shuffle the cards." The Dean returned to England, and obtained another commission, but while his vessel was wind-bound at the waterside, the news reached

him that the bloody Queen was *dead*, and that the Protestants of Ireland were saved. And so delighted was Queen
Elizabeth, when she heard of it, that she settled a pension of
forty pounds per annum, for life, upon Elizabeth Edmonds,
by whose instrumentality God had graciously preserved her
Protestant subjects in Ireland.—Mant 1, 250.

CHAPTER VIII.

THE REFORMATION.

THE last chapter brought us up to the reign of good Queen
Elizabeth, under whose auspices the Reformation progressed
rapidly. The Protestant services were restored in the Irish
churches ; and, so indignant were the Papists at this, that
they resolved to work a miracle in Christ Church Cathedral,
Dublin, before the Lord-Deputy, the Archbishop, and the
Privy Council.

The Cathedral contained a marble image of Christ, with a
reed in His hand and a crown of thorns on His head ;
while service was going on blood was seen to run through
the crevices of the crown of thorns, and to trickle down the
face of the crucifix. The Papists cried out, " See, our
Saviour's image sweats blood." Some of the terrified poor
people fell before the image, prayed to it, and counted their
beads. They were told that " Jesus could not but sweat blood
when heresy was brought into His Church." The service
broke up ; the people smote their breasts ; but the Archbishop
of Dublin directed the sexton to wash the image, and see
if it would bleed afresh. It was immediately found that a
sponge, saturated with blood, had been placed over the head

of the image, within the crown of thorns; and in process of time, the blood soaked through upon the face.

Such is a Popish miracle! and whenever we hear of a Popish miracle, we may be sure that it is produced in a somewhat similar way. The Archbishop caused the image to be destroyed, though originally erected by himself; and, upon the following Sunday, preached upon the text, " God shall send them 'strong delusions that they should believe a lie." Of this sermon Mant says, " The Archbishop exposed the cheats who openly stood there, with Father Leigh, upon a table before the pulpit, with their hands and legs tied, and the crime written upon their breasts. This punishment they suffered three Sundays, were imprisoned for some time, and then banished from the realm. This (pretended miracle) converted above one hundred persons present who swore they would never hear mass more."* Archbishop Curwen wrote the particulars of it to the Archbishop of Canterbury (Parker), who was glad thereof, by reason that the clergy were debating at the time whether images should stand in the churches or no; the Queen herself being indifferent in this matter, but rather inclinable to them. But this letter which the Archbishop showed her, wrought her consent for the throwing of the images out of the churches; together with many texts of Scripture which our Archbishop and other divines had laid before her for the demolishing of them. The occurrence at Christ Church had also no doubt a great effect on the Lord-Deputy of Ireland, and probably quickened his activity in re-establishing the use of the English liturgy.† The incident we have just recorded in the Irish Reformation had some effect in promoting the good cause in England, for this Romish plot recoiled upon its authors, and the Reformation progressed

* Mant 1, 256.   † *Ibid.*

more vigorously than before. The circulation of the word of God became very great. The English liturgy was restored. The English Articles of Religion were published. A.D. 1592, the Irish University, Trinity College, Dublin, was founded, and *the Reformation was effected with the approval of all the bishops of Ireland, except two.* These two were William Walsh, Bishop of Meath, and Thomas Laverhouse, Bishop of Kildare. The people showed their anxiety to understand and receive the new doctrine; and it is recorded in A.D. 1558, that 7,000 Bibles had been sold in Dublin within two years. A large Bible was placed in each of the Dublin Cathedrals, Christ Church and St. Patrick's, and many came to read and hear their contents.

In fact, Ireland promised to become a Protestant nation, when unhappily the Act of Uniformity (2 Elizabeth c. 2) was passed, which decreed that the revised English Liturgy, as contained in the *Second* Prayer-book of King Edward, should be used in all the churches in Ireland, and that in cases where the minister did not read English, the services were to be in Latin. This was as inconsistent as impolitic, for the Church of England teaches in its Twenty-fourth Article, that " it is a thing plainly repugnant to the Word of God, and the custom of the primitive Church, to have public prayer in the church, or to minister the sacraments, in a tongue not understanded of her people." This suicidal enactment may be truly said to have done more to impede the Gospel in Ireland, than all the opposition of the Papacy.

The Pope, indeed, on his part, was not idle, but made several efforts to recover his lost ground, and to overthrow the English rule.* Amongst other acts he encouraged Irish rebels, gave them his blessing; and pardoned several troops

---

* For many instances of this see Mant i. 285, 307.

of Italian robbers, on condition that they should go and fight
for the Papal cause in Ireland.

In the year 1580, Pope Gregory XIII. granted to all the
Irish who would fight against Queen Elizabeth the same
plenary pardon and remission of all their sins as were
granted to those who were engaged in the holy war against
the Turks.*   Consequently, successive rebellions took place
in Ireland, by means of which the country, but more especially the Church, was reduced to the utmost extreme of
wretchedness.   After a final struggle at Kinsale, in the
County of Cork, in which the rebels, together with their
Italian and Spanish allies, were defeated, the country became somewhat quiet; but famine, pestilence, and misery
ensued.

The following dreadful description by the poet Spenser,
A.D. 1580, of the famine which followed those several
rebellions, will recall to the memories of some many a
heartrending description of Ireland in later years.   He
says :—

"*Ireland was a most rich and plentiful country, yet, ere
one year and a half, they were brought to such wretchedness,
as that any stony heart would rue the same.   Out of every
corner of the woods and glens, they came creeping forth upon
their hands, for their legs would not bear them : they looked
like anatomies of death ; they spake like ghosts coming out
of the graves ; they did eat the dead carrions, happy where
they could find them, yea and one another soon after : inas-
much as the very carcases they spared not to scrape out of
their graves : and if they found a plot of watercresses or
shamrocks, they flocked as to a feast for a time, yet not able
to continue there withal : so that in short space there was*

* Cox, "History of Ireland," i. 365, quoted in Mant i. 307.

*none almost left, and a most populous and beautiful country
suddenly left void of man or beast."* Such (adds Mr. King)
were the blessings procured by the bulls of the Pope, for his
deluded and infatuated victims.

The above facts, then, make it clear that at the Reformation no new Church was planted in Ireland, but that the Irish
Church simply threw off the errors which had crept into her
bosom of late, and returned to the ancient Scriptural faith
of her early days. How senseless, then, is it for politicians
to speak of the injustice of taking the property of the
Romanist and transferring it to the Protestant. There never
was such a transfer ; there never was a Royal Act by which
such a transfer was made. Let our readers remember this
when we proceed hereafter to deal with the property and
income of the Established Church in Ireland.

CHAPTER IX.

ESTABLISHMENT OF A SECOND CHURCH IN IRELAND.

In the previous chapters we have traced up Ireland's Ecclesiastical history from the days of the apostles to the seven-
teenth century, and, as our readers must have observed,
perhaps with surprise, that during the whole of that period,
no second Church, no second set of bishops, or clergy, had
ever been heard of in Ireland.

But the great subject of controversy in Parliament and
out of Parliament at present is the existence of two Churches
in Ireland, and the real question which the Parliament
of Great Britain is called up on to decide really is whether

one of these Churches shall be swept away, so far as human instrumentality can do it.

Strange, too, it is, that the Church which Protestant England is asked to destroy is not the modern Church of Rome, which, as our readers have seen, brought such woe and calamity into Ireland, but the Church endangered is Ireland's good old Scriptural Church, one with England and Scotland in faith and doctrine.

How did this second Church arise ? How can we explain its existence? If good Queen Bess had imitated Bloody Mary's example, and burnt or driven into banishment the Roman Catholic bishops of Ireland, and installed new Protestant bishops in their stead, we could readily understand the matter. Had she seized upon the ancient cathedrals and other churches of Rome in Ireland, expelled the Roman Catholic worshippers, and forcibly turned them into Protestant churches, we could at once see the almost needs-be of an opposition establishment. But Elizabeth did neither, she simply left the clergy and laity to please themselves, and the Irish bishops, whom the Pope had himself approved, renounced Popery, cast off the Pope's supremacy, and became Protestant bishops. The clergy, as a rule, did the same, and the people followed their example ; and thus, through the recognized and lawful bishops of Ireland, the Irish cathedrals, and other churches, once more became Christian and Protestant temples. The Church of Ireland did not separate from her lawful bishops and set up unlawful ones ; but she followed her lawful bishops in their renunciation of Romish idolatry, and in their return to Scriptural truth. So that, through all the darkness which enveloped the once glorious Church of Ireland, she can prove that she is *not a new Church*, that her bishops are not usurping bishops, but that she is, substantially, that ancient Church in which St. Patrick laboured, and which the illustrious Columba adorned, as our readers have seen.

In addition, the Irish Church, whose destruction is now sought, can prove (what Rome's bishops in Ireland cannot prove) that her bishops are the regular successors of the earliest bishops of Ireland; * but above all, with God's Holy Word, and our scriptural reformed Liturgy in hand, she can show that she is pre-eminently that Church in Ireland which is apostolic in doctrine and discipline, which holds up Christ the Son of God as the sinner's hope, and proclaims to all, of every creed, salvation through His saving name.

And here it is well to say a word or two regarding the large body of Presbyterians in Ireland who, though differing as to form of worship, hold with the United Church in matters of faith.

In 1610 King James I., who had succeeded Elizabeth, sent over a large number of English and Scotch colonists, who received grants of land which had been forfeited on account of the frequent rebellions in which the owners had been engaged, and which were lying waste and uncultivated, and were very thinly inhabited. Of these colonists some were members of the Church of England, but the greater number were Presbyterians. Thus were formed what was called the Ulster plantation, and the property, for the most

---

* To show how little room there is for dispute on this point, Mant says, vol. i., p. 270, " Even the Popish prelates, so long as any of them survived who were in their sees before the Reformation, were ready to assist at the consecration of Protestant bishops: that the true Episcopal character of the hierarchy of the Irish Church is unquestioned and unquestionable, and protected against all exception even from the Papists themselves."

part, was invested in certain London companies, now known by the name of the Irish Society.

Mant thus describes the transaction,—" The rebellions having been brought to a close, A.D. 1608, some of the rebels were outlawed, and their lands, situate in the northern counties of Ireland (equivalent to 818,344 acres English statute measure), were forfeited to, and thus left at the disposal of, the Crown. Of these 335,680 acres, of like measure, were assigned for 'the Londoners and other undertakers' on the special agreement that 'they should not suffer any labourer that would not take the Oath of Supremacy (to the English Crown) to dwell upon their lands.' The building of Derry was, in accordance with the agreement, commenced A.D. 1611, and completed by the Londoners A.D. 1617, whence its compound appellation, London-Derry.

These Presbyterians, thus brought into Ireland, continued for awhile in partial conformity to the Established Church, and it was not until the year 1642 that they began to set up their own Church government and discipline. The first presbytery was formed at Carrickfergus in June, 1642, which was composed of Presbyterian army chaplains and lay "elders" chosen from Scotch regiments recently sent into Ireland.

In following out the history of the Irish Church we must not omit to mention a very injudicious measure enacted by King James, which practically placed the masses of the Irish people under the influence and control of the Romish priests, who, educated at foreign seminaries, and encouraged by the mistakes made by the English Government, began to appear in large numbers. By James's mistaken enactment the people were freed from the rule of their own native lords, and made free to act as they liked; all which would have been very well if the people had been first taught how to use their liberty. But they were not, and therefore became the victims of rebellious priests and agitating demagogues. It was an evil hour for Ireland which invested the priests with this influence over the People.

Still, something more was needed to give the Church of Rome the *appearance* of a Church in Ireland, of which she was now destitute, for her own Bishops and clergy had deserted her, and embraced their native Church, now once more independent of apostate Rome ; so that the Pope was left, literally, without an organized Church or Episcopal body in Ireland.

What, then, did he do ? What *could* he do, but *form a new Church, and establish a new Episcopate? And this he did.*

Other Bishops were gradually appointed by the Pope to assume the titles and authority of the lawful Bishops who had embraced the Reformation, and to bring together all persons whom they could persuade to abandon the national Church and join the new sect.

In the year A.D. 1614 the Roman Catholic clergy held what is called the Synod of Drogheda, the first Synod of the new Church. We need not detail its proceedings ; it is sufficient to observe that by it, and Councils of a similar character, held in other provinces, *an entirely new communion was formed in Ireland.*

This is admitted by an eminent Roman Catholic writer (O'Sullivan), who candidly admits that, in the year 1621, all the Irish Sees were filled by " ringleaders of heresy," *i e*, by Protestants, and that in that year there were only four Roman Catholic Bishops, two of whom lived in foreign countries.

Such was the origin in Ireland of that Romish Church which falsely claims to be the Church of St. Patrick, and of the ancient Saints of Ireland.

The two succeeding chapters will be devoted to the present position and dangers of the Church, as threatened by Mr. Gladstone's iniquitous Resolutions.

———

CHAPTER X.

PRESENT POSITION.

THERE are many interesting features in the modern history of the Irish Church, which must be passed over very briefly, because we propose to devote this last chapter to details regarding the present income and property owned by the Establishment, respecting which such enormous exaggerations have been put forth.

Had space permitted, we might have dwelt on the terrible massacres of Protestants which from time to time have stained the sod of Ireland with human blood; but this topic will be more aptly dealt with in the succeeding chapter, which will be devoted to the question of whether the Irish Church has failed in her mission.

Much that is interesting might be laid before our readers regarding the state of Ireland at the time of the Commonwealth, which is thus described by Carlyle, Cromwell's apologist and panegyrist, who says, in his own strange style— " *Ireland, ever since the Irish Rebellion broke out and changed itself into an Irish massacre, in the end of 1641, has been a scene of distracted controversies, plunderings, excommunications, treacheries, conflagration, of universal misery and blood and bluster, such as the world before or since has never seen. The history of it does not form itself into a picture, but remains as a huge blot and indiscriminate blackness, which the human memory cannot willingly charge itself with."* After describing the various parties contending for the mastery, Carlyle adds, *" All these plunging and tumbling in huge discord, for the last eight years, have made of Ireland and its affairs the black unutterable blot we speak of."*

Something we might say too of the many eminent men who in God's good providence have been raised up from time to time in Ireland's Church—of Jeremy Taylor, of worldwide fame; of Bramhall, and Bishop Bedell, the translator of the Old Testament into Irish, and who was so beloved by the people that even a Popish Priest exclaimed over his grave, " Anima mea sit cum Bedello,"—" May my soul be with that of Bedell;" but we must pass on, and as we can only give a cursory sketch, need only remind our readers of the time of James II., who lost his crown for his attempts to re-establish Popery in England; and of William, of immortal memory, who gained his crown by coming forward to maintain "the liberties of England and the Protestant religion;" of the last struggle of James in Ireland, and the victories of William of Orange ; of the siege of Derry, the romantic incidents of which are told with such thrilling interest by Charlotte Elizabeth ; of the never-to-be-forgotten battle of the Boyne, and that of Aughrim. Instead of these moving tales of flood and field, we must now draw our readers' attention to the comparatively dull details of the income, &c., of the Irish Church.

Parliamentary returns enable us to calculate, with some degree of certainty, the Church revenues in Ireland. The total annual available income is 540,379*l*., out of which the Ecclesiastical Commissioners' fund is 111,937*l*., and from which salaries of clerk and sexton, church requisites, repairs of buildings, &c., have to be provided; thus relieving the laity from these burdens. The Archbishops and Bishops receive altogether 55,110*l*. per annum; on the average 3,628*l*. Then comes the income of the beneficed clergy (1,510 in number) with 245*l*. each, out of which the salaries of the curates have to be paid.

The above total sum is derivable from glebe lands and tithe rent-charge, which last amounts to 401,114*l*. a-year, the whole of which is paid by the landlords, and eight-ninths of it by Protestants, leaving only a ninth that comes to the clergy through Roman Catholic landlords. The whole is a sum less than the annual income of at least one English nobleman, and considerably less, as Sir Robert Peel lately remarked, than the cost of one of our ironclads.

The whole of the tithe rent-charge possessed by ecclesiastical persons is less than a hundredth part of the produce of the soil.

This tithe-rent charge in Ireland is a composition for tithe, and is of the nature of a reserved rent, *which never belonged to either landlord or tenant*.

The glebe lands contain 132,756 acres; some of them were granted to the clergy of the Church of Ireland for ever by the native princes of Ireland during their primitive independence of all foreign supremacy. *They were never granted for the benefit of the Church of Rome.* For example, the Bishop of Meath holds lands granted to Keiran, Bishop of Cloumacnoise (now united to Meath) in the sixth century. The property of the monasteries of modern foundation, *i.e.*, since the twelfth century, is not possessed by the

Irish Church, but by lay proprietors, who now receive over 81,000*l.* a year from this source.

Let it always be remembered that the Church of Rome claimed no jurisdiction till many centuries after the time when these grants began to be made, and by far the most valuable of them, which lie in the north, were original grants from the Crown *to the Reformed Church* at the time of the plantation of Ulster in 1608-9, as shown in a previous chapter.

Moreover, the Church in Ireland owes a considerable portion of her present endowments to the exertions and munificence of her Bishop since the Reformation. Dr. Hook, in his Life of Archbishop Bramhall, relates that in four years that prelate recovered about 40,000*l.* a year to the Church, which had been wasted or impropriated. Primate Boulter left 30,000*l.* for the augmentation of small benefices. Primate Robinson left a large sum for the same purpose.

The inviolability of the Irish Church was guaranteed at the time of the union (in the year 1800) of the two countries, by the 5th Article of the Act of Union, which runs thus :—
" That the Churches of England and Ireland, as now by law established, be united into one Protestant Episcopal Church, to be called ' The United Church of England and Ireland,' and that the doctrine, discipline, and government of the said United Church shall be, and shall remain in full force for ever, as the same are now by law established for the Church of England ; and that the continuance, and preservation of the said United Church, as the Established Church of England and Ireland, shall be deemed and taken to be an essential and fundamental part of the Union."

To this Parliamentary guarantee we add the additional security afforded by the Queen's Coronation Oath, which runs thus :—

The Archbishop of Canterbury, addressing Her Majesty, said :—

" Will you solemnly promise and swear to govern the people of this United Kingdom of Great Britain and Ireland, and the dominions thereto belonging, according to the Statutes in Parliament, agreed on, and the customs of the same ? "

Queen.—" I solemnly promise to do so."

Archbishop.—" Will you, to your power, cause law and justice, in mercy, to be executed in all your judgment ? "

Queen.—" I will."

Archbishop.—" Will you, to the utmost of your power, maintain the laws of God, the true profession of the Gospel, and the Protestant Reformed Religion established by law ? And will you preserve and maintain inviolably the settlement of the United Church of England and Ireland, and the Doctrine, Worship, Discipline, and Government thereof, as by law established within England and Ireland, and the territories thereunto belonging ?

" And will you preserve unto the Bishops and Clergy of England and Ireland, and to the United Church committed to their charge, all such rights and privileges as by law do or shall appertain to them or any of them ? "

Queen.—" All this I promise to do."

The Queen then proceeded to the Communion Table, and laying her right hand on the Holy Gospel in the great Bible tendered to her by the archbishop, *kneeling* and *uncovered*, took the Oath, saying these words :—" The things which I have here promised I will perform and keep ; So help me God."

Very much more might be added regarding the property of the Church in Ireland, but we trust that enough has been adduced to prove·—

1. That the Church holds her property by a title at least as good as that of any lay estate in Ireland or England.

2. That it has been formally and solemnly guaranteed by the State.

———

CHAPTER XI.

HAS THE IRISH CHURCH BEEN A FAILURE?

ACCORDING to promise, we propose in this, the closing chapter of the Irish Church history, to make some remarks on the statement so often made by the enemies of the Church, that its history proves that it has been a *great failure*. Like all other charges, however, preferred against the Irish Church, the more it is examined, the more clearly will it be seen to be *utterly groundless*.

For instance, " Mr. Gladstone, in opening the debate in the House of Commons on this subject, invited attention to certain statistics relative to the comparative numbers of Roman Catholics and Protestants in 1672, and contrasted this with the number of the two parties at the present time. In 1672 there were 800,000 Roman Catholics, and 300,000 Protestants, in Ireland, whereas at the present time the Roman Catholics are more numerous when compared to the Protestants than they were then. This is supposed to be a crushing argument against the Irish Church.

" It is affirmed on the authority of these statistics, that Protestantism in Ireland will be best promoted by disestablishing and disendowing the Irish Church. We are persuaded that a more careful examination of these figures will furnish an unanswerable argument against our opponents, and in our favour. It is true that there were, in 1672,

800,000 Roman Catholics, and 300,000 Protestants, or eight Romanists to three Protestants. Mr. Gladstone omits to state that of these 300,000 Protestants, 200,000 were Nonconformists, and 100,000 members of the Irish Church. It will therefore be seen that the Roman Catholics were as eight to one when compared to the members of the Established Church; whereas now, they are only six and a half to one. This, therefore, is a decided gain to the cause of the Church of Ireland. The Roman Catholics are 4,500,000, whilst the members of the Established Church are close upon 700,000.

" Again, the Nonconformists in 1672 were 200,000, the members of the Established Church 100,000 ; that is, the former were two to one compared with the latter. In 1861, the members of the Established Church were 700,000, the Nonconformists only 600,000, and yet we are told that these figures prove the utter uselessness of an Established Church. The Nonconformists have lost ground immensely, both in respect of Roman Catholics and Episcopalians. We repeat, the Roman Catholics in 1672 were as eight to one compared to the members of the Established Church, now they are only six and a half to one. In the same year, the Nonconformists were two to one as compared to the members of the Established Church, whilst now they are only as six to seven, that is, they are actually fewer by 100,000. Yet, strange to say, we are calmly told by those who would disestablish and disendow the Irish Church, that their scheme, if crowned with success, would advance the Protestant cause.

" In support of the same view we have heard a great deal about the marvellous increase of Protestant Dissenters in Ireland, between 1834 and 1861. In the former year we are told there were less than 22,000, whilst in the latter

they exceeded 76,000, or had increased by 251 per cent.
Here again, however, an examination of the figures will
prove that so far from having increased, there was a positive
decrease of 22 per cent.! No one is charged with the in-
tention of misrepresenting the facts of the case, the dis-
crepancy arises from the different way in which certain
bodies of Nonconformists were classified in the census reports
of 1834 and 1861. For example, 45,000 Methodists who
were reckoned as members of the Established Church in the
former report, are classified as Protestant Dissenters in the
latter report. Other deductions of a smaller character have
to be made, and when made shew that there were 4,890
fewer, or, as before stated, there was a positive decrease of
22 per cent. It is worthy of observation that the decrease,
though greatly felt amongst all the religious bodies of Ireland
between 1834 and 1861, was felt least by the Established
Church. The decrease of the entire population was 27 per
cent.; the Roman Catholics lost 30 per cent.; the Protestant
Dissenters 22 per cent.; the Presbyterians 18 per cent.;
whilst the Established Church lost only 13 per cent. Where,
then, is the evidence that the Irish Church has been so
great a failure that it should be suddenly deprived of the
position which it has occupied the last 300 years? It is also
worthy of observation that the Independents and Baptists of
Ireland do not together number 9,000. This is not a fact
calculated to recommend the voluntary system.

" The misstatements and misrepresentations on the subject
seem to be positively endless. A paper has been circulated
in which it was stated that there are 199 parishes in Ireland
in which there is not a single member of the Irish Church.
Whilst in one sense this is correct, it is positively untrue as
understood by the vast majority of those who hear and read

it, as will be seen by a few words of explanation:—There are two kinds of parishes in Ireland, the civil and the ecclesiastical, but which are by no means conterminous; whilst there are two thousand four hundred and twenty-eight civil parishes, there are but fifteen hundred and ten ecclesiastical benefices,—so that in some of the ecclesiastical parishes there are two, three, and even as many as seven, civil parishes. There is one civil parish which contains only forty square yards. Whilst it is true that there are 199 civil parishes in which there are no members of the Established Church, there is *only one* ecclesiastical parish without members of the Established Church.

"Now, what is the impression conveyed to the vast majority of those who hear or read the statement that there are 199 parishes without any members of the Established Church? Clearly this: that there are 199 clergymen without any people to whom they are called to minister. Now there is only one parish, committed to the care of a clergyman, that has no members of the Established Church. Is it therefore right—is it indeed honest—to speak of 199 parishes as possessing no members of the Established Church, withholding the explanation above given of the two kinds of parishes in Ireland?"

Before we leave this part of the subject, we may surely ask that if the Irish Church is a *great failure*, how it has happened that in West Connaught, in the last thirty years, the congregations have increased from thirteen to fifty-seven, and the churches from seven to thirty, through the missionary efforts of the Irish Church amongst the Roman Catholics?

The following figures prove incontestably that the Irish Church, instead of being a failure, has made remarkable progress of late years.

Progressive increase of clergy, &c., in Ireland from 1730 to 1863:—

	Clergy.	Churches.	Benefices.	Globe houses.
1730	800	400	...	141
1806	1,253	1,029	1,181	295
1826	1,977	1,192	1,396	768
1864	2,172	1,579	1,510	978

The fact of the Protestants of Ireland being in a minority has been mainly owing to the persecutions they have suffered at the hands of the Romish Church. One or two instances will suffice. In the year 1641, it was calculated by Sir John Temple, an ancestor of Lord Palmerston, and others, that 300,000 Protestants were massacred or expelled from Ireland: and from despatches of the Lords Justices of this period, the English were told "*that Popery will never rest satisfied with toleration, or even equality, but must ever strive after ascendency, even through torrents of blood.*" Sir John Temple, one of the Privy Council, says that, "*From the priests went out the watchword, both of time and place*" [*for the massacre*].

In James II.'s time the Irish Protestants suffered extreme persecution. Five lists of attainder were published, comprising nearly all the Protestant nobility and ladies, and it was made highly penal for Protestants to attend a place of worship, or even to meet in greater numbers than two or three, on any pretence whatever.

In 1798 an awful massacre of Protestants took place; Priest Murphy, one of the rebel leaders, refused to spare the life of a Protestant at Gorey, county Wexford, declaring "that where there was but *one drop* of Protestant blood in a family they ought to be put to death."

Between the years 1826 and 1834 it is computed that no

less than 175,000 Protestants, disheartened and discouraged by the undue preference given to Romanists, emigrated to America. In Canada alone there are 500,000 adult male Irish Protestants—in part emigrants from Ireland—as a whole the progeny of the Irish Church. It is not, then, rather a wonder that there are so many Protestants still remaining in Ireland, and who represent two-thirds of the talent, wealth, manufactures, and enterprise of the whole country?

One word in conclusion as to the propriety of maintaining the Protestant Church in Ireland, although it be the Church of a minority of the population. Nothing that we can say on this point can be so effectual as the following words which fell from Mr. Gladstone himself in the House of Commons in 1835:—

" I deny," said Mr. Gladstone, " that this (the conversion of the Roman Catholics) was the exclusive business of the Church of Ireland. One great part of its mission was the instruction of those who belonged to it in the maxims of religion, loyalty, and truth. Has it failed in that respect? or are they not, on the contrary, to be reckoned among the most loyal and devoted subjects of the Crown? England is a Protestant State, she ought, therefore, to uphold the Protestant religion. What does that mean? That while we respect the antiquity and the practices of the Church of Rome, we also assert the right of private judgment, and the independence of the human mind."

CHAPTER XII.

SUMMARY OF HISTORICAL FACTS.

1. PREVIOUS to the English invasion, 1171, the Irish Church was unconnected with Rome. This is acknowledged by Pope Adrian IV. in his celebrated Bull, dated 1155, and afterwards by Pope Alexander III.

2. At the Synod of Cashel, in 1172, the Bishops under the influence of Henry II., acknowledged the supremacy of the Bishop of Rome for the first time.

3. Many Irish Bishops held aloof; and it was not till near the middle of the 13th century that the Pope was able to interfere in the appointment of the Archbishop of Armagh.

4. Between the reigns of Henry II. and Henry VIII., while all Ireland was nominally Roman Catholic, there was a more bitter feeling between the English and Irish parties than there ever has been at any period since the Reformation.

5. During this period much land was given by the nobles and knights for monasteries and abbeys, and the tithes and glebes belonging to the different parishes were added to these endowments, on condition that the abbots appointed vicars to do the duty on receiving one-third of the tithes.

6. In the reign of Henry VIII. the Irish Church abjured the supremacy of the Pope, continued to do so during the reign of Edward VI., again submitted for a time under Mary, and finally abjured it under Elizabeth, in 1558.

7. All the bishops, with two exceptions, remained in their sees, the priests generally remained in their parishes, and the people attended their parish churches for the first eleven years of Elizabeth's reign.

8. The bishops so conforming consecrated their suc-

cessors, from whom are descended the present bishops of
the Irish Church, who can trace their descent from the Church
of St. Patrick in the fifth century.

9. The present Roman bishops in Ireland can trace no con-
nection with the Ancient Irish Church. There is no record of
the two nonconforming bishops—who were forced by Queen
Mary into sees that were already occupied—ever taking part
in the consecration of a bishop for Ireland.

10. Whatever property rightfully belonged to the Irish
Church previous to the time of Henry II., rightfully be-
longs to the present Irish Church as her legitimate suc-
cessor.

11. The Abbey lands given in the time of her connexion
with Rome were all given to laymen by Henry VIII., and
not an acre was given to the Church.

12. On the contrary, the tithes and glebes which properly
belonged to the Church were also seized, and are now in the
possession of the Duke of Devonshire, the Earl of Donough-
more, Mr. Herbert of Mucross, and numberless others, to the
amount of £80,000 a year in tithes alone, independent of
the glebes.

13. At the Reformation, two great changes took place in
the Churches of Europe. Rome, and those which remained
connected with her, adopted a new creed—that of Pope
Pius IV.—first published in 1564, six years after the Reformation had been completed in England, while the English,
Irish, Scotch, and the Protestant Churches on the Continent
retained the ancient creeds—the Apostles' and Nicene—and
wiped away the incrustations of false doctrines that had been
gradually creeping over the face of the Church, but which
were not to be found in the Bible.

14. The Churches of England, Ireland, and Scotland

never held the new creed of Pope Pius, which every one now joining the Roman Church must acknowledge as his creed.

15. Thus, both by succession of bishops, and by holding the same creeds, the present Irish Church is the representative of that which refused to acknowledge the Roman supremacy previous to the time of Henry II.

16. If the Roman Church has any claim, it is only to the Abbey lands given previous to Henry VIII., not one acre of which, as we have already stated, is in possession of the Church of Ireland. They are all in lay hands.

17. The cause of the preponderance of Romanists in Ireland is not difficult to discover. From the time of Henry II. the Irish habits, manners, and language were prescribed within the English pale. In the early part of Elizabeth's reign, the clergy were forbidden to use the Irish language, though the people understood no other; and if the clergyman did not understand English, he might pray and preach in Latin, but not in Irish!

18. The Bishop of Rome took advantage of this mistake, and sent bishops and priests into Ireland to draw away the people from the ancient Church.

19. This was not till after he had given up all hopes of the Queen acknowledging his supremacy. Had she done so, he was ready to allow the mass to be in English, and would grant other favours, in a great measure confirming the Reformation; but on her persisting in her refusal, he issued a bull of excommunication, absolved her subjects from their allegiance, and stirred up Philip of Spain to invade England with the "Invincible Armada."

20. Since the Reformation, the greater portion of the property of the Irish Church has been added, and all con-

firmed to her. Out of 132,000 acres of glebe land, 111,000 were granted in Ulster by James I. Every landed proprietor in Ireland who pays tithe rent-charge, received, derived, or purchased his property subject to the charge. .

21. The incomes of the clergy have been so reduced within the last forty years, that they do not now amount to more than one-half the amount paid at that time.

22. The Church property had been so reduced in the time of Henry VIII. and his successors by the rapacity of the nobles, that in order to afford a decent maintenance for a clergyman several parishes had constantly to be united into one benefice. Hence, while there are 2,428 nominal or civil parishes in Ireland, there were some years ago but 1,100 benefices; and even now, after many pluralities have been done away with, they number but 1,510.

23. This explains the statement that there are 199 parishes in Ireland without a Protestant—a statement true to the ear but false to the sense, as 145 of these are connected with benefices which have hundreds and some of them over a thousand Protestants in them; 32 of them are in the hands of the Ecclesiastical Commissioners, and pay nothing to a clergyman: 3 more will be so at the deaths of the present incumbents; 18 never paid anything to a clergyman; and only one has a paid incumbent with a church, but the church is not without a congregation, as persons in the adjoining parishes attend the service every Sunday.

24. Some of the parishes so spoken of are so small, that one is covered by a tan-yard, another by a brewery, another is but forty yards square, and of some the exact locality is unknown.

25. Formerly every farmer in Ireland paid tithe in kind'; and taking his farm subject to this charge, he got his land at

a reduced rent. The inconvenience of this mode of payment led generally to an amicable arrangement between the clergyman and his parishioners, and the tithe was commuted for a money payment.

26. In 1824, by Goulbourn's Act, the clergyman and his parishioners were permitted to make this commutation compulsory for twenty-one years, subject to a revision every seven years, according to the price of corn. In the great majority of parishes this was carried out.

27. Subsequent Acts made this commutation compulsory in every parish, and repealed the law by which, if the valuation of the parish increased or diminished, it could be altered at the end of twenty-one years.

28. In 1838 another law was passed amalgamating the tithe composition with the rent, in which it has been included ever since, and paid to the landlord, who, when handing it over to the clergyman, was entitled to retain five shillings out of every pound for his trouble.

29. By the Tithe Composition Act of 1824 the clergy lost about one-third of their incomes; by that of 1838 another fourth was deducted, thus reducing them in the last forty years by one half.

30. By an Act of the Irish Parliament in the last century doing away with the tithe of agistment, or that on grazing land, it is generally thought that more than one-half the then Church property was taken away.

31. When the spoliations of the olden times are taken into account, together with the conduct of the Irish Parliament in the last century and the two great Tithe Acts of the present, it will not surprise any to hear that the Irish Church, instead of receiving, as many think she does, the whole tithe property of Ireland, meaning thereby the tenth part of the produce of

the land, receives in tithe rent charge only the 120th part of the produce, or the twelfth part of the tithe.

32. By far the larger proportion of the glebe lands now in possession of the beneficed Clergy of Ireland, has been given by Protestants for Protestant purposes. The whole of the glebe lands amount to 132,756 acres, of which no less than 111,151 acres are grants to the Church since the Reformation, so that it is clear that five-sixths of the present glebe lands of the Irish Church never belonged to the Church of Rome.

33. The revenues of the Irish Church so far from being in excess, would, if equally divided, give an average income to Incumbents of 245*l.*, out of which the salaries of Curates would have to be paid; while of the total rent charge, amounting to 401,114*l.* per annum, 370,000*l.* are paid by Protestant landlords, leaving only 30,000*l.* to be paid by Roman Catholic landlords who have purchased their estates subject to this liability.

www.ingramcontent.com/pod-product-compliance
Lightning Source LLC
Chambersburg PA
CBHW021523090426
42739CB00007B/747